GOLD MINE in a suitcase

EARN MONEY AT HOME
A BEGINNERS BOOK FOR LEARNING
SCREEN PRINTING

EXPLAINED IN DETAIL HOW, ON A SMALL BUDGET, YOU CAN SCREEN PRINT REAL JOBS AT HOME IN YOUR GARAGE, OR BASEMENT. YOUR STARTUP MATERIALS WILL ALL FIT IN A SUITCASE.

by ROBERT J. LICHER SR.

Robert Licher
Gold Mine in a Suitcase
     Earn Money at Home, Silkscreen Printing on a Low Budget

www.goldmineinasuitcase.com

1st Edition
Includes Index

ISBN: 1496133838
Printed in the United States of America by CreateSpace

1 Authorship – Marking

2 Authorship – Title

TABLE OF CONTENTS

CHAPTER ONE 1
Introduction, What you can accomplish on a small budget – with cartoon pages of explanation

CHAPTER TWO 5
How to build a simple set up, material sources board, screen, squeege, hinges, hold up stick

CHAPTER THREE 15
Coating a screen with photo emulsion using a simple v-shaped coater

CHAPTER FOUR 21
A job comes in and you do it – Bumper stickers are printed with easy, detailed instructions

CHAPTER FIVE 43
Building a simple screen exposure unit to make photo screens

CHAPTER SIX 51
Building an inexpensive one color shirt printer

CHAPTER SEVEN 65
Printing a t-shirt using our t-shirt printer

CHAPTER EIGHT 73
How to clean and reclaim a screen for another job

CHAPTER NINE 79
Services, materials, diploma

CHAPTER TEN 83
Printing a color job

**DEDICATED TO MY WIFE,
JACQUELINE**

ACKNOWLEDGEMENTS

My sincere thanks to Jacqueline Licher — Jack of all Trades, Gina Flores — Computer Coach, all my sign painter friends, Ken Zimmerman, Jersey Joe, Tom Clark, Joe Anohos, Sal at Dayton West, McLogan's Sign Supplies in L.A., Willie White — Sign Painter, Joe Pina and Don Martinez.

CHAPTER ONE

WHAT YOU CAN ACCOMPLISH ON A SMALL BUDGET

THE GOLD IS HERE!

It's in this book,

It's in your hands,

It's in your home...

Lacquer Print on water Gelatin Size decal

Print enamel on red plastic sticker material and die cut to shape

Lacquer printing on water slide off decals for toys

Enamel printing on clear plastic with a sticky back

Show card display for counter top and table menu

Screen Print T-Shirts

AFTER YOU LEARN THESE SIMPLE STEPS...

the list is endless...

NOVELTIES

T-SHIRTS

STATIONERY

DISPLAY CARDS

LABELS

TOY DECALS

PACKAGING

The market is endless... everyone that does something or makes a product needs cards, sign, decals, labels, boxes, and displays.

Screen printing lets you do these jobs with very little equipment, and very little space — a garage, room, basement or even your kitchen table.

CHAPTER TWO

WE BUILD OUR LOW-PRICED PRINTING SET-UP

TOOLS...

**To dig a ditch,
saw a board,
or silk a screen,**

you need TOOLS

GETTING STARTED

Turn the page for pictures and a list...

PRINTING BOARD WITH SCREEN FRAME LOCATED ON THE CENTER OF THE 24" x 32" PRINTING BOARD

WOODEN 19" x 22" SCREEN FRAME
With 180 Mesh

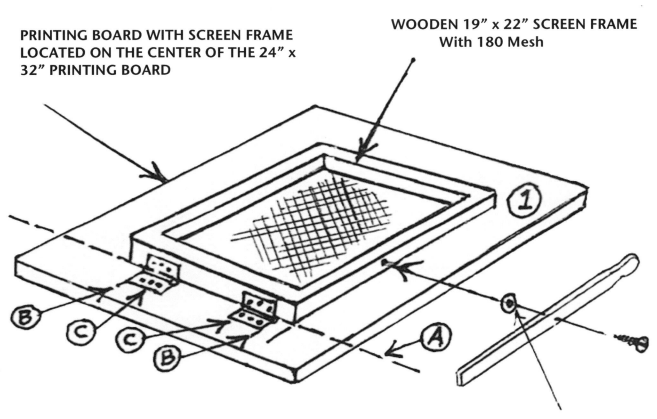

WASHER
LARGE PAINT STICK
1" WOOD SCREW
Predrill a 1/16" hole in the center of the paint stick and the center of the frame.

DRAW LINE (SEE A) USING A BLACK MARKER ACROSS THE BASE OF THE SCREEN FRAME. MARK A LINE ONE INCH IN FROM THE CORNER (SEE B). TWO HINGES WILL LAY FLAT ON THAT LINE (SEE C).

THINGS WE NEED TO BUILD A PRINTING BOARD

BASE PLATE SINK CUT OUT OR A PIECE OF EXT PLYWOOD 24" x 32" x ¾" $12.00*

TWO 2 ½" STEEL OR BRASS HINGES, WITH WOOD SCREWS

HEAVY DUTY PAINT MIXING STICK WITH A WOOD SCREW AND WASHER

13 ½" SQUEEGE $25.00*

WOODEN SILK SCREEN FRAME 19" x 22" COVERED WITH 180 TO 200
MONOFILAMENT $25.00*

*prices are approximate

Order Screen and Squeege from McLogan Silkscreen Supplies
On the web at http://www.mclogan.com

2010 South Main St., Los Angeles, CA 90007

Phone: (213) 749-2262

Ask for the Order Desk – and don't forget to ask for a catalog.
They have all different kinds of paint and supplies.

WHEN A KITCHEN CONTRACTOR BUILDS A COUNTER THAT HAS A SINK, HE CUTS A HOLE IN THE COUNTER FOR THE SINK. THE PIECE HE CUTS OUT IS CALLED THE SINK CUT OUT. AS LONG AS THE SINK CUT OUT IS LARGER THAN OUR SILKSCREEN FRAME (19" x 22"), WE CAN USE IT FOR OUR PRINTING BOARD. IT HAS A FORMICA TOP, SO THAT'S GOOD. USUALLY THE CONTRACTOR WILL SELL YOU A CUT OUT BOARD FOR A NOMINAL FEE, HE MAY EVEN GIVE IT TO YOU.

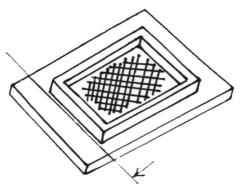

PLACE THE 19" x 22" SCREEN FRAME ON THE CENTER OF THE 24" x 32" SINK CUT OUT PRINTING BOARD. MARK THE PRINTING BOARD WITH A LAYOUT LINE TO SPOT THE HINGES.

RIGHT SIDE (FLAT)

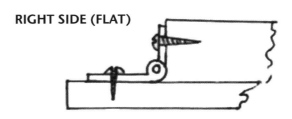

LAY THE HINGES ON THEIR "FLAT SIDE" AGAINST THE SCREEN FRAME. HOLD THE HINGES TO THE SCREEN FRAME WITH A "C" CLAMP. THEN PRE-DRILL THE SCREW HOLES WITH A 1/16" DRILL.

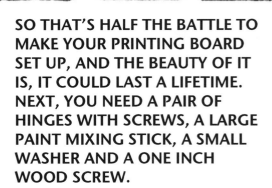

SO THAT'S HALF THE BATTLE TO MAKE YOUR PRINTING BOARD SET UP, AND THE BEAUTY OF IT IS, IT COULD LAST A LIFETIME. NEXT, YOU NEED A PAIR OF HINGES WITH SCREWS, A LARGE PAINT MIXING STICK, A SMALL WASHER AND A ONE INCH WOOD SCREW.

DRILL A 1/16" HOLE IN THE CENTER OF A LARGE PAINT MIXING STICK. USE A WOOD SCREW AND A WASHER TO POSITION IT ON THE LEFT SIDE OF THE SCREEN.

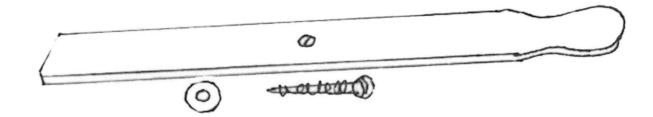

THIS SHOWS THE HOLD UP STICK ATTACHED TO THE SIDE OF THE SCREEN FRAME.

WE NEED A TEMPORARY REST FOR THE SQUEEGE SO IT WON'T FALL OVER WHEN WE LIFT THE SCREEN AFTER THE PRINTING STROKE. CUT A 10" x 10" PIECE OF CORRUGATED CARDBOARD FROM A BOX.

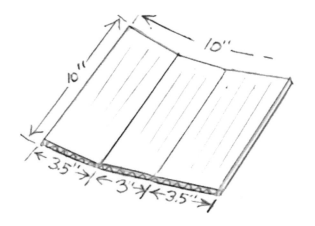

CUT THE CORRUGATED CARD SO THE FLUTES GO WITH THE BEND.

AFTER PRINTING A JOB, YOU CAN REMOVE THE STAPLES AND SAVE THE BOARD.

STAPLE THE CARDBOARD REST TO THE BOTTOM (HINGE END) OF THE SCREEN

AFTER STAPLING OR NAILING THE CARD TO THE FRAME, TAPE THE TOP.

OUR LOW PRICED SET UP

**SCREEN HINGED TO A PRINTING BOARD
WITH A SQUEEGE READY TO PRINT**

READ THIS BOOK — THEN REMEMBER THIS...

TO GET STARTED AND MAKE MONEY, YOU ONLY NEED THE BASIC PRINTING BOARD, SCREEN AND SQUEEGE, PLUS THE INK.

DON'T WORRY ABOUT THE SCREEN PREPARATION. IF YOU GET THE ART FROM THE CUSTOMER, SEND IT TO GEORGE AND FRANCISCO IN LOS ANGELES, CA. THEY MAKE THE SCREENS THAT ARE READY TO USE FROM THE ART YOU SEND THEM.

LATER, I'LL SHOW YOU HOW TO EXPOSE AND DEVELOP YOUR OWN SCREENS.

TRY TO GET ONE COLOR JOBS TO START — LIKE BUMPER STICKERS AND T-SHIRTS.

BOB

Exposed to Art
15828 S. Broadway, Unit #D
Gardena, CA. 90248
(310) 965-1902

THE WORLD'S CHEAPEST PRINTING PRESS !!

INTRODUCING

WITH YOUR HELP, HE FORCES PAINT THRU A SCREEN
STENCIL TO MAKE ONE – OR ONE THOUSAND – PIECES !!

SO LET'S GET STARTED... IN THREE SHORT WEEKS, YOU WILL HAVE A NICE SET UP

- SET OF HINGES
- PAINT STICK W/SCREW
- SCREEN FRAME
- SQUEEGE
- EMULSION COATER
- PHOTO EMULSION

- SINK CUT OUT (2)
- 2 FOAM PIECES
- PIECE GLASS
- EXACTO KNIFE
- AMBER LITH FILM
- QUART ENAMEL BLACK

- QUART ENAMEL RED
- RAGS
- SHO CARD
- LACQUER THINNER
- MINERAL SPIITS

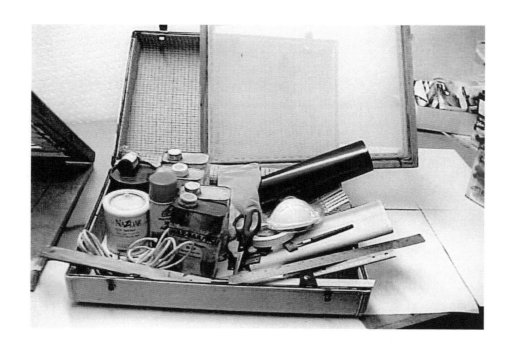

PICTURE OF THE SUITCASE WITH ALL THE EQUIPMENT YOU NEED

CHAPTER THREE
COATING EMULSION ON THE SCREEN

WHEN YOU BUY YOUR "SILK SCREENS" (ACTUALLY MONOFILAMENT), McLOGANS WILL HAVE WOODEN 19" x 22" FRAMES COVERED WITH 180-200 MESH COUNT FOR AROUND $25.00 EACH.

THIS CHAPTER WILL DISCUSS HOW TO COAT OUT THE SCREEN WITH PHOTO LIGHT SENSITIVE EMULSION. WHEN DRY, THE SCREEN CAN BE LOCKED UP IN A EXPOSURE FRAME WITH THE FILM POSITIVE ART IN POSITION. THEN, EXPOSE THE SCREEN TO THE SUN'S POWERFUL ENERGY. NEXT, TAKE THE SCREEN TO THE SINK — A GENTLE SPRAY OF WATER WILL WASH OUT THE UNEXPOSED EMULSION. DRY THE SCREEN IN THE SUN, TOUCH UP AND THE SCREEN IS READY TO PRINT.

THE EMULSION WILL BE LIGHT SENSITIVE AFTER YOU MIX THE ACTIVATOR, SO "PULL DOWN THE SHADES" AND DO THE SCREENS AND COATING IN A SEMI-DARK ROOM. THE LEFTOVER EMULSION SHOULD GO IN THE REFRIGERATOR. DON'T LET THE EMULSION FREEZE.

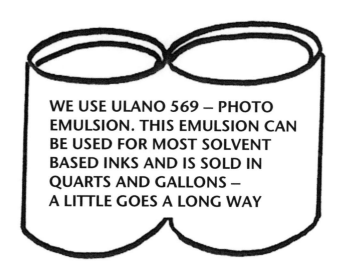

WE USE ULANO 569 – PHOTO EMULSION. THIS EMULSION CAN BE USED FOR MOST SOLVENT BASED INKS AND IS SOLD IN QUARTS AND GALLONS – A LITTLE GOES A LONG WAY

CAUTION!!

EMULSION COMES WITH AN ACTIVATOR POWDER IN A SMALL DARK PLASTIC JAR. PUT ON A MASK BEFORE YOU OPEN THE JAR. THE VERY FINE ACTIVATOR POWDER IS NOT GOOD TO BREATHE – SO ADD THE PRESCRIBED WATER SLOWLY. CAP IT TIGHT AND SHAKE UNTIL IT ALL TURNS TO A LIQUID.

MASK – DON'T BREATHE THE ACTIVATOR POWDER

ADD WATER

ONCE THE ACTIVATOR IS A LIQUID, IT IS MORE STABLE. OPEN THE EMULSION CONTAINER AND SLOWLY POUR IN THE ACTIVATOR. MIX WITH A CLEAN PAINT STICK. NOW THE EMULSION IS ACTIVATED AND READY TO COAT A SCREEN. FROM NOW ON, THE EMULSION HAS TO BE IN A REFRIGERATOR. DON'T FREEZE. PUT A DANGER STICKER ON THE CONTAINER.

KEEP OUT OF BRIGHT LIGHT.

SCREEN COATING STEPS

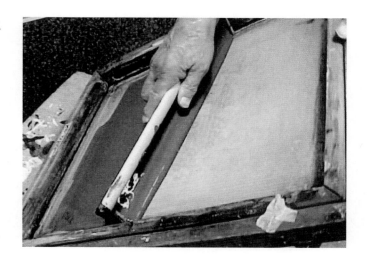

- POUR THE EMULSION IN THE COATER
- HOLD THE SCREEN ON A 60° ANGLE
- COAT THE INSIDE OF THE SCREEN FABRIC USING GENTLE PRESSURE WHILE PULLING THE COATER UP. AS YOU REACH THE TOP, TILT THE COATER UP.
- TURN THE SCREEN OVER AND COAT THE PRINTING SIDE. THEN TURN THE SCREEN OVER AND COAT THE INSIDE SURFACE (THIS WILL FORCE THE EMULSION THRU THE SCREEN SO THE PRINTING SURFACE WILL HAVE A THICKER COAT).
- AFTER THE EMULSION IS DRY, ADD ONE MORE COAT TO THE OUTSIDE SURFACE.
- STACK UNDER A FAN TO DRY.
- WHEN DRY, THE SCREEN IS READY TO "SHOOT" (EXPOSE).
- KEEP THE SCREEN IN A COOL, DARK ROOM UNTIL IT IS READY TO "SHOOT"

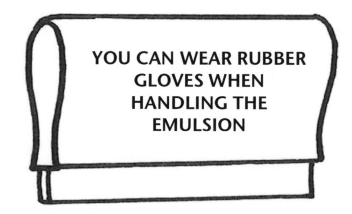

YOU CAN WEAR RUBBER GLOVES WHEN HANDLING THE EMULSION

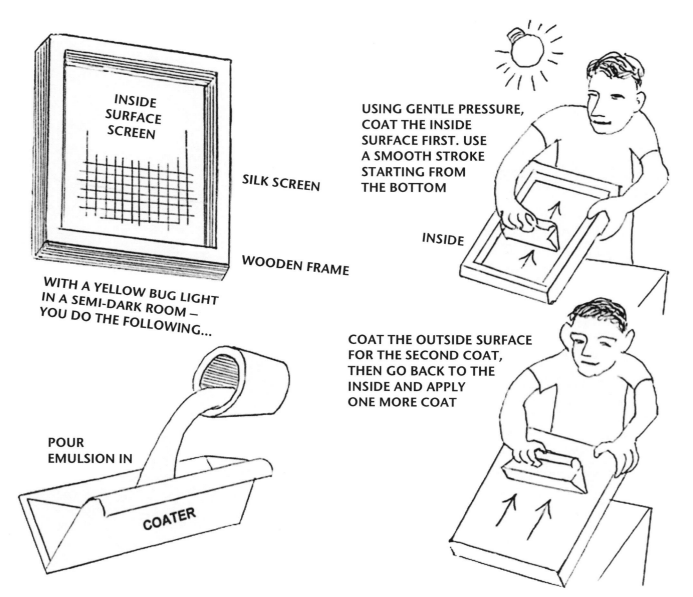

INSIDE SURFACE SCREEN

SILK SCREEN

WOODEN FRAME

WITH A YELLOW BUG LIGHT IN A SEMI-DARK ROOM – YOU DO THE FOLLOWING...

POUR EMULSION IN

COATER

USING GENTLE PRESSURE, COAT THE INSIDE SURFACE FIRST. USE A SMOOTH STROKE STARTING FROM THE BOTTOM

INSIDE

COAT THE OUTSIDE SURFACE FOR THE SECOND COAT, THEN GO BACK TO THE INSIDE AND APPLY ONE MORE COAT

AFTER THE EMULSION IS DRY, ADD ONE MORE COAT TO THE OUTSIDE SURFACE AND STACK UNDER THE FAN. WHEN DRY, THE SCREEN IS READY TO "SHOOT". (BE EXPOSED)

AFTER COATING THE SCREEN, FIRST INSIDE AND THEN OUTSIDE, AND THEN ONCE MORE INSIDE, STACK THE FRAMES TO DRY ON WOODEN BLOCKS IN A DARK ROOM WITH A FAN.

IMPORTANT
THE LAST INSIDE COAT FORCES AN EVEN THICKER COAT OF EMULSION TO THE OUTSIDE SURFACE OF THE SCREEN. THE OUTSIDE SURFACE IS THE PRINTING SIDE.

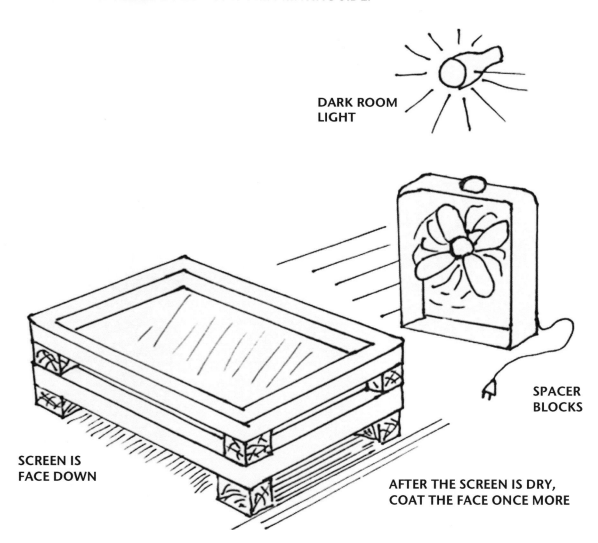

DARK ROOM LIGHT

SPACER BLOCKS

SCREEN IS FACE DOWN

AFTER THE SCREEN IS DRY, COAT THE FACE ONCE MORE

CHAPTER FOUR

WE PRINT SOME BUMPER STICKERS

WE KEEP THEM SMALL TO FIT INSIDE A BUSINESS ENVELOPE
SMALL CARS – SMALL BUMPERS – CHEAP TO MAIL

SILK SCREEN PRINTING IS A MISNOMER BECAUSE WE USE POLYESTER MATERIAL AS A SCREEN FOR OUR PURPOSES. IT IS A LOT STRONGER AND DOES NOT ABSORB MOISTURE LIKE SILK.

A CUSTOMER BRINGS YOU A LAYOUT FOR A BUMPER STICKER. HE WANTS ONE COLOR ON A WHITE BACKGROUND. IT'S FOR A TRAVEL AGENCY. HE HAS SAME SIZE ART, BLACK AND WHITE, BUT NO FILM. TAKE THE ART TO KINKO'S, STAPLES OR A SIMILAR STORE OR STUDIO.

ASK FOR A FILM TRANSPARENCY. IN SCREEN PRINTING "YOU GET WHAT YOU SEE". SO IF THE FILM IS CLEAR WITH DARK LETTERS, THAT IS HOW IT WILL PRINT. THEY CALL THE FILM IMAGE A TRANSPARENCY. WE USE IT TO EXPOSE OUR SILK SCREEN.

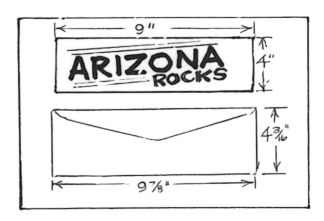

THE BUMPER STICKER HAS TO FIT IN A BUSINESS SIZE ENVELOPE.

KEEP YOUR COATED SCREENS IN A COOL DARK ROOM UNTIL IT IS EXPOSURE TIME. EVEN THEN, PULL DOWN THE SHADES. YOU NEED A SEMI-DARK ROOM WHILE YOU PLACE THE FILM POSITIVE ON THE SCREEN AND INTO THE EXPOSURE FRAME.

FOR PRINTING A BUMPER STICKER THAT IS 4" x 9" x 3", OUR SCREEN SET UP WILL PRINT THREE AT A TIME. WE NEED SIX IMAGES (FILM), BECAUSE SOME TRANSPARENCIES FROM ELECTRONIC PRINTERS ARE NOT OPAQUE OR DARK ENOUGH. CUT THE TRANSPARENCY TO SIZE.

CUT THE CORNERS OF THE TOP PIECE FOR THE TAPE

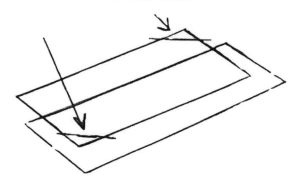

SCOTCH-TAPE ONE FILM ON TOP OF THE OTHER (TWO LAYERS). USE A LIGHT TABLE OR WINDOW TO LINE THEM UP. NOW THEY SHOULD BE DARK ENOUGH.

MAKE A LAYOUT ON A CARD SO YOU CAN SCOTCH-TAPE THE THREE IMAGES (DOUBLE LAYERED)

TAPE ALL THREE TOGETHER

TAKE THE COATED SCREEN AND THE FILM POSITIVE. POSITION THE POSITIVE ON THE PRINTING BOARD "RIGHT READING". LEAVE ROOM AT THE END FOR PAINT AND THE BEGINNING PAINT STROKE OF THE SQUEEGE.

BUTT THE SCREEN INTO THE HINGES. BRING THE SCREEN DOWN ON THE FILM. RUB THE SCREEN WITH YOUR FINGERS TO STICK THE SCOTCH-TAPE TO THE OUTSIDE SURFACE OF THE SCREEN, HOLDING THE FILM IN PLACE.

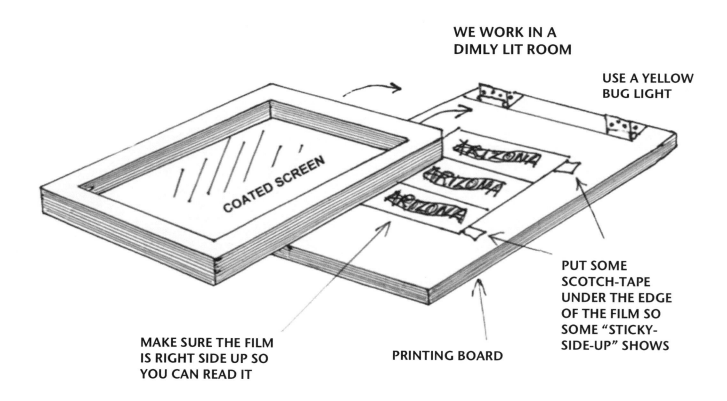

WE WORK IN A DIMLY LIT ROOM

USE A YELLOW BUG LIGHT

COATED SCREEN

PUT SOME SCOTCH-TAPE UNDER THE EDGE OF THE FILM SO SOME "STICKY-SIDE-UP" SHOWS

MAKE SURE THE FILM IS RIGHT SIDE UP SO YOU CAN READ IT

PRINTING BOARD

24

NOW YOU HAVE A FILM POSITIVE AND YOU CAN "SHOOT" A SCREEN.

UNDER A YELLOW LIGHT CONDITION, LAY THE FILM FACE UP ON THE PRINTING BOARD, CENTERED SO YOU CAN READ IT. PUT SOME SCOTCH-TAPE UPSIDE DOWN (STICKY SIDE UP) UNDER THE CORNERS OF THE FILE — LETTING IT STICK OUT BY AN INCH.

ON THE PRINTING BOARD, BUMP THE SCREEN INTO THE HINGES. NEXT, LOWER THE SCREEN ONTO THE FILM.

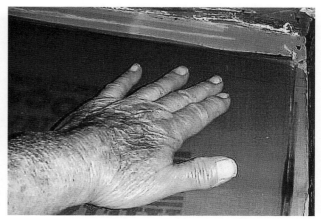

PRESS DOWN ON THE SCREEN SO THE FILM STICKS TO THE SCREEN.

LOOK UNDER THE SCREEN WITH THE FILM TAPED TO THE PRINTING SIDE.

I USED MASKING TAPE SO YOU COULD SEE THE TAPE.

FRAME WITH FILM IN PLACE.

EXPOSURE BOARD WITH FOAM BOARD GLUED IN PLACE WITH BLACK SHO CARD.

PUT THE SCREEN ON THE EXPOSURE BOARD. THE FOAM AND SHO-CARD BASE HAVE TO BE TALLER THAN THE FRAME.

CLOSE THE GLASS FRAME OVER THE SCREEN AND LOCK IN PLACE.

COVER THE GLASS WITH SHO-CARD OR THIN PIECE OF MASONITE.

GET IT OUT INTO THE BRIGHT SUN. UNCOVER AND EXPOSE FOR 60 TO 90 SECONDS.

USE A YELLOW BUG LIGHT
IN A SEMI-DARK ROOM TO
DO THE FOLLOWING:

LOOK IT OVER

WITH THE FILM STUCK IN PLACE
(BY THE SCOTCH-TAPE), POSITION
THE SCREEN OVER THE EXPOSURE
BOARD. BRING THE GLASS DOWN
OVER THE SCREEN FACE. LOCK IN
PLACE. LAY A PIECE OF SHO-CARD
OVER THE GLASS. CARRY IT OUT
INTO THE SUN. PLACE IT FACE UP
ON A BOX OR TABLE. LIFT THE
SHO-CARD AND LET THE BRIGHT
SUN SHINE ON THE IMAGE FOR A
MINUTE AND A HALF. THEN COVER
IT WITH THE CARD AND TAKE IT
BACK INSIDE.

YELLOW BUG LIGHT

COATED SCREEN

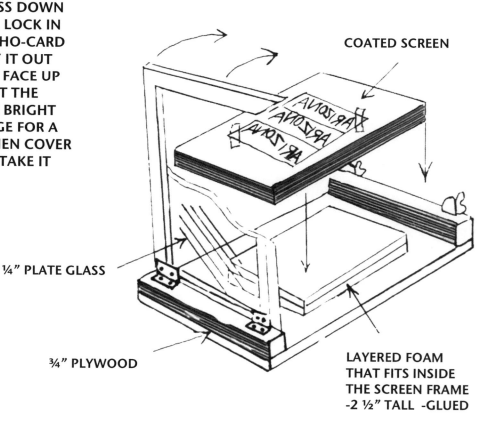

¼" PLATE GLASS

¾" PLYWOOD

LAYERED FOAM
THAT FITS INSIDE
THE SCREEN FRAME
-2 ½" TALL -GLUED

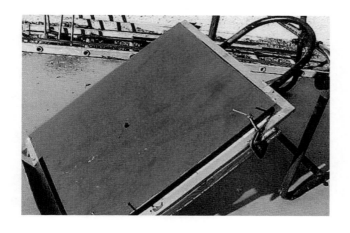

COVER IT UP, GO INSIDE AND TAKE THE SCREEN OUT.

REMOVE THE FILM AND GO TO THE SINK, BATH OR SHOWER.

WITH A GENTLE SPRAY OF WATER, SPRAY BOTH SIDES OF THE SCREEN. THE EMULSION NOT EXPOSED WILL WASH OUT.

WHEN THE IMAGE IS CLEAR, BLOT WITH NEWSPRINT AND PUT OUT IN THE SUN TO DRY.

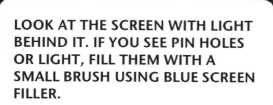

LOOK AT THE SCREEN WITH LIGHT BEHIND IT. IF YOU SEE PIN HOLES OR LIGHT, FILL THEM WITH A SMALL BRUSH USING BLUE SCREEN FILLER.

IT IS WATER SOLUBLE.

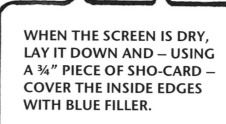

WHEN THE SCREEN IS DRY, LAY IT DOWN AND — USING A ¾" PIECE OF SHO-CARD — COVER THE INSIDE EDGES WITH BLUE FILLER.

FILL IN THE EDGES OF THE SCREEN WITH
BLUE BLOCK-OUT USING A PIECE OF CARD.

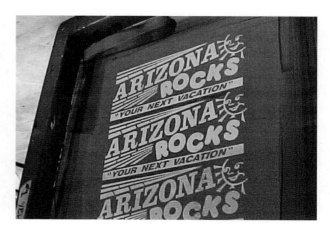

USE A PIECE OF SHO CARD TO SMEAR THE
BLUE BLOCK-OUT FILLER AROUND.

TURN THE SCREEN OVER AND BLOCK OUT
THE OTHER SIDE (JUST THE EDGES).

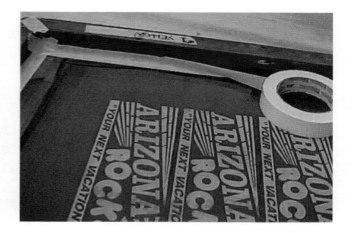

WHEN DRY, USE MASKING TAPE ON ALL
FOUR INSIDE EDGES.

OUR BUMPER STICKER SHEETS CUT TO SIZE WILL PRINT THREE AT A TIME.

A COATED OUT SCREEN WITH A FILM POSITIVE OF OUR BUMPER STICKER.

PLACE THE FILM POSITIVE ON THE PAPER — WHERE WE WILL PRINT.

TAPE TWO CORNERS OF THE FILM DOWN ON THE PAPER.

THIS IS HOW THE FILM POSITIVE LOOKS ON CENTER OF PAPER.

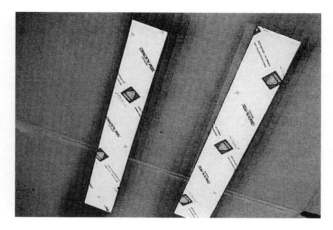

CUT TWO PIECES OF THE STICKER STOCK AND SPRAY WITH SPRAY STICK.

CUT A PIECE OF MANILA FOLDER AND TAPE IT TO THE SET UP STICKER.

PRINT ALL KINDS OF FLAT STOCK... BUMPER STICKERS, CONVENTION BADGES, CAR AND TRUCK SIGNS, OPEN AND CLOSED SIGNS, IRON ON TRANSFERS FOR CAPS AND T-SHIRTS, DECALS FOR TOYS, LIQUOR DISPLAYS, AND MUCH MORE.

BRING THE SCREEN DOWN AND LINE UP THE BLACK COPY WITH THE SCREEN.

IT SHOULD LOOK LIKE THIS... DON'T MOVE THE COPY AND LIFT THE SCREEN.

TAPE THE CORNERS OF THE COPY TO THE PRINTING BOARD.

MARK THE EDGES OF THE COPY SO WE CAN MASK IT OUT FOR A STICKEM SPRAY.

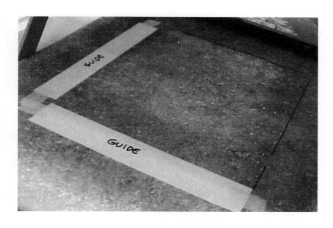

TAKE THE TWO GUIDES YOU SPRAYED AND TAPE THEM ON THE BOTTOM AND SIDE.

WE ARE GOING TO SPRAY THE PRINTING AREA – SO WE NEED TO MASK IT OFF.

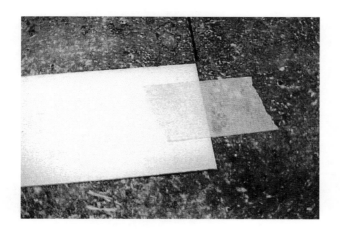

USING WIDE PAPER OR NEWSPRINT, MASK OFF THE PRINTING AREA.

SPRAY THE PRINTING AREA WITH ANY LIGHT SPRAY ADHESIVE.

REMOVE THE NEWSPRINT AND PUT YOUR SET UP PAPER AGAINST THE GUIDES.

WHEN YOU PRINT EACH PIECE, THE SPRAY STICK WILL HOLD THEM DOWN.

AFTER PRINTING, THEY WILL COME UP EASILY.

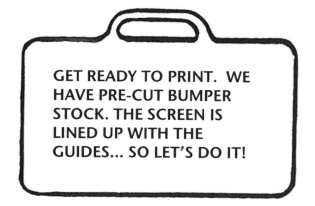

GET READY TO PRINT. WE HAVE PRE-CUT BUMPER STOCK. THE SCREEN IS LINED UP WITH THE GUIDES... SO LET'S DO IT!

PUT YOUR FIRST BLANK PIECE
AGAINST THE GUIDES.

AFTER THE PIECE IS IN PLACE, LIGHTLY
PRESS IT DOWN. CHECK HANDS FOR
PAINT.

BRING THE SCREEN DOWN —
READY TO PRINT.

PUT PAINT ON THE HINGED END
OF THE SCREEN.

LIFT THE SCREEN AND LIGHTLY PULL THE
PAINT OVER THE SCREEN TO CHARGE IT.

BRING THE SCREEN DOWN AND
PRESS DOWN WITH THE SQUEEGE.

PULL THE SQUEEGE TOWARD YOU IN A
SMOOTH PRINTING STROKE.

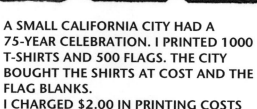

A SMALL CALIFORNIA CITY HAD A
75-YEAR CELEBRATION. I PRINTED 1000
T-SHIRTS AND 500 FLAGS. THE CITY
BOUGHT THE SHIRTS AT COST AND THE
FLAG BLANKS.
I CHARGED $2.00 IN PRINTING COSTS
FOR EACH ITEM. I MADE $3000 IN ONE
WEEK (LESS SCREEN PREP AND PAINT).
YOU CAN DO IT TOO!

SLANT THE SQUEEGE ON AN ANGLE
LIKE A SNOW PLOW.

AT THE END OF THE PRINTING STROKE, LIFT
THE SCREEN AND PUSH THE PAINT FOR A
FLOOD COAT.

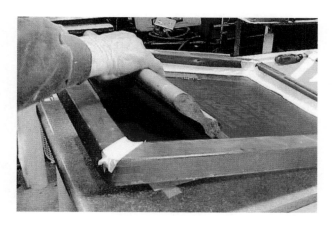

THIS WILL CHARGE THE SCREEN FOR THE
NEXT PRINTING STROKE.

HOLD THE SQUEEGE AT THIS ANGLE FOR THE FLOOD COAT.

LIFT THE SCREEN. THE SPRAY ADHESIVE HOLDS THE PRINTED PIECE IN PLACE.

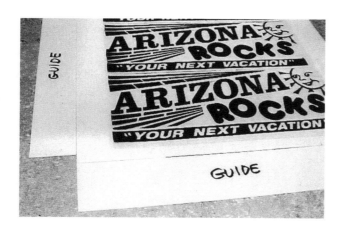

LIFT THE SCREEN — AND VOILA — YOU HAVE THREE BUMPER STICKERS.

PUT YOU HOLD-UP STICK IN POSITION AND TAKE OUT THE FINISHED PRINT.

OUT SHE COMES !!

HANG THEM UP TO DRY WITH WOODEN SNAP CLOTHES PINS.

YOU CAN HANG THEM BACK TO BACK

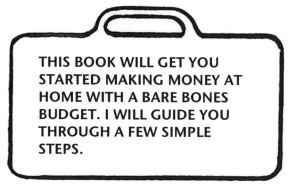

THIS BOOK WILL GET YOU STARTED MAKING MONEY AT HOME WITH A BARE BONES BUDGET. I WILL GUIDE YOU THROUGH A FEW SIMPLE STEPS.

CHAPTER FIVE
BUILDING A SCREEN EXPOSURE FRAME

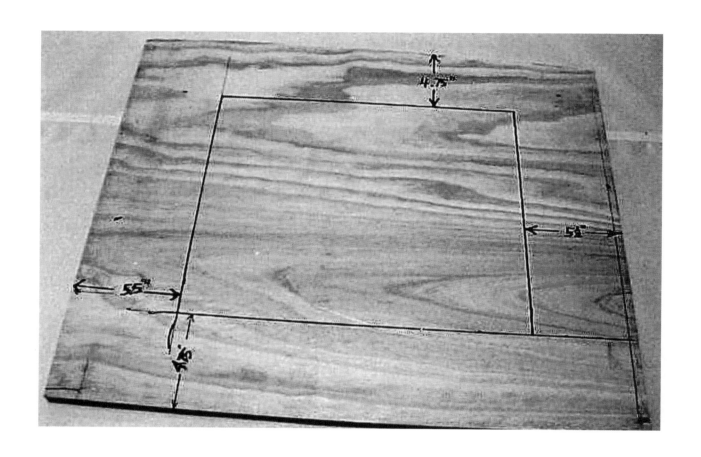

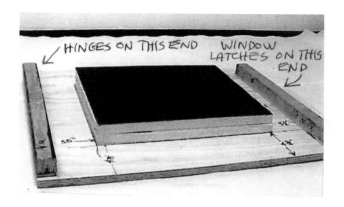

ADD A PIECE OF GLASS AND YOU HAVE A SCREEN EXPOSURE BOARD

GLUE TWO PIECES OF WOOD 2" SQUARE BY 24" LONG TO BOTH ENDS OF THE BOARD

DON'T USE LIQUID NAILS FOR GLUEING THE
FOAM - IT MELTS THE FOAM.

THE HINGED WINDOW HOLDS DOWN THE FILM POSITIVE AGAINST THE COATED SCREEN. WHEN WE MOVE THE UNIT OUT IN THE SUN, THE GLASS HAS TO HAVE HINGLES ON ONE END AND WINDOW HOLD-DOWN LATCHES ON THE OTHER END. AN ALUMINUM CHANNEL FRAME (4 PIECES) WILL BE GLUED IN PLACE TO GET THIS DONE. ADD TWO HANDLES (ONE ON EACH END).

BUILD AN ALUMINUM FRAME AROUND THE ¼" PLATE GLASS. POP-RIVET TWO HINGES TO ONE END OF THE ¼" ALUMINUM CHANNEL. THEN GLUE THE GLASS IN THAT CHANNEL. GLUE THE CHANNEL TO THE LAST THREE SIDES OF THE GLASS. WHEN THE SCREEN IS POSITIONED OVER THE FOAM BLOCKES, THE HINGED WINDOWS CLOSES DOWN AND LOCKS IN PLACE WITH THE SCREEN AD FILM POSITIVE SCOTCH-TAPED TO THE SCREEN INSIDE. COVER THE GLASS WITH A CARD AND CARRY OUT TO THE SUN.

MATERIAL LIST FOR SCREEN EXPOSURE UNIT

ONE PIECE OF ¾" THICK EXTERIOR PLYWOOD 24" x 34"
ONE PIECE OF ¼" PLATE GLASS 22" x 32"
TWO PIECES OF 1" THICK FOAM 1" x 14 ½" x 17"
ONE TUBE OF LIQUID NAILS & APPLICATOR GUN ** DON'T USE ON FOAM BLOCKS
ONE SQUEEZE BOTTLE OF ELMER'S WOOD GLUE
TWO 2" HINGES
SMALL BOX OF POP-RIVETS WITH DRILL ** BIT SAME SIZE AS RIVETS
POP-RIVET GUN
TWO WINDOW LATCHES WITH WOOD SCREWS
TWO PIECES OF 2" SQUARE WOOD, 22" LONG
TWO PIECES ¼" ALUMINUM CHANNEL, 22" LONG
TWO PIECES ¼" ALUMINUM CHANNEL, 32" LONG
TWO METAL HANDLES WITH SCREWS

FINISHED EXPOSURE FRAME WITH
BLACK SHO CARD FOR A COVER
WHILE YOU CARRY IT OUT FOR
EXPOSURE.

READY TO GO OUT IN THE SUN –WITH CARRYING HANDLES

THE SCREEN EXPOSURE UNIT IS LIKE A BOOK. YOU LIFT THE COVER (GLASS FRAME WITH ALUMINUM CHANNEL) WITH TWO HINGES ON ONE END. THE OTHER END OF THE FRAMED GLASS HAS TWO WINDOW LATCHES TO LOCK THE "BOOK" SHUT. INSIDE ARE TWO FOAM BLOCKS THAT THE SCREEN RESTS ON. THE FILM ART POSITIVES ARE ON THE SCREENS PRINTING SURFACE. CLOSE THE "BOOK", LOCK IT WITH THE WINDOW LATCHES, COVER THE GLASS WITH A CARD, TAKE THE UNIT OUT INTO THE SUN, UNCOVER THE GLASS FACE — EXPOSING THE SCREEN TO THE SUN FOR ONE AND ONE-HALF MINUTES. COVER THE GLASS, TAKE IT INSIDE, REMOVE THE SCREEN, AND TAKE OFF THE FILM ART. WASH OUT THE UNEXPOSED EMULSION FROM THE SCREEN WITH A GENTLE SPARY OF WATER, LET DRY IN THE SUN TO HARDEN THE EMULSION. TOUCH UP ANY PIN HOLES — READY TO PRINT.

HINGE ONE END OF THE ALUMINUM CHANNEL. LAY A 2" HINGE AGAINST THE CHANNEL. MARK AND DRILL HOLES FOR POP-RIVETS ON EACH END OF THE CHANNEL. USE A DRILL BIT THE SAME SIZE AS THE RIVETS. AFTER THE HINGES ARE SECURE, GLUE THE GLASS IN THE CHANNEL. THEN ADD THE OTHER THREE CHANNELS.

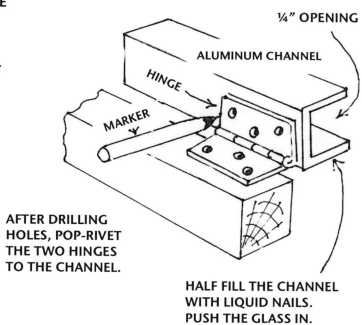

¼" OPENING

ALUMINUM CHANNEL

HINGE

MARKER

AFTER DRILLING HOLES, POP-RIVET THE TWO HINGES TO THE CHANNEL.

HALF FILL THE CHANNEL WITH LIQUID NAILS. PUSH THE GLASS IN.

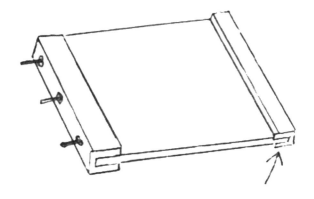

CUT A PIECE OF LIGHT CHANNEL.
GLUE IT TO THE OTHER END OF THE GLASS.

ON THE HINGE END OF THE FRAME,
REMOVE THE NUTS AND BOLT THE
HINGE IN PLACE.

USING LIQUID NAILS, GLUE A PIECE OF ALUMINUM CHANNEL TO BOTH SIDES OF THE GLASS.

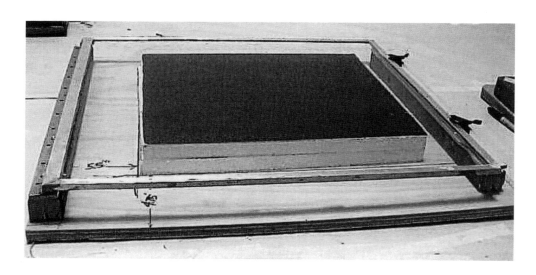

48

FIRST THING... MARK YOUR BOARD!

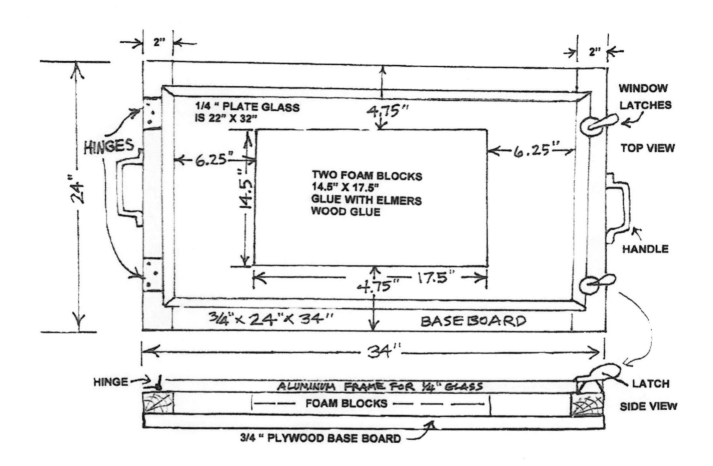

2"

HINGES

24"

1/4 " PLATE GLASS
IS 22" X 32"

4.75"

6.25"

14.5"

TWO FOAM BLOCKS
14.5" X 17.5"
GLUE WITH ELMERS
WOOD GLUE

6.25"

4.75"   17.5"

3/4"x 24"x 34"

BASE BOARD

2"

WINDOW
LATCHES

TOP VIEW

HANDLE

34"

HINGE →

ALUMINUM FRAME FOR ¼" GLASS

FOAM BLOCKS

3/4 " PLYWOOD BASE BOARD

LATCH

SIDE VIEW

CHAPTER SIX

WE BUILD A T-SHIRT PRINTER

THIS SHIRT PRINTER CAN ALSO BE USED AS A BASIC SCREEN PRINTER FOR BUMPER STICKERS, LABELS, OR ANY FLAT STOCK.

IT'S MAIN PURPOSE IS TO PRINT T-SHIRTS.

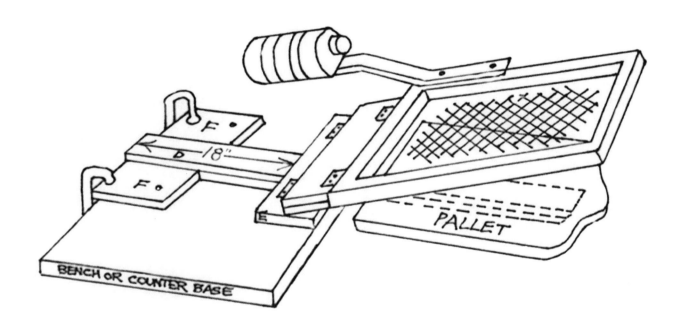

PARTS INCLUDE ¾" EXTERIOR PLYWOOD, BASIC HINGES, HARDWARE, ANGLE BRACKETS, AND SOME NAILS AND SCREWS. GET A HANDY FRIEND TO ADVISE AND HELP. THIS IS SIMPLE CONSTRUCTION. THE DEVICE WILL LAST A LIFETIME PRINTING T-SHIRTS AND FLAT STOCK.

TO GET START WITH LESS EXPENSE,
BUY A SMALLER SIZE OF ¾" PLYWOOD.

GET PIECES "C", "D", & "E" PLUS
"F", "G" AND "H". (SEE DIAGRAM)

IF YOU GO TO LOWES OR HOME DEPOT, THEY WILL CUT THE PLYWOOD TO THE SPECS ON THIS PAGE.

C = SHIRT PRINTER
D = SHIRT PRINTER
E = HINGE BASE
F = FOOT (SHIRT PRINTER)
G = SCREEN HOLDER
H = SCREEN HOLDER

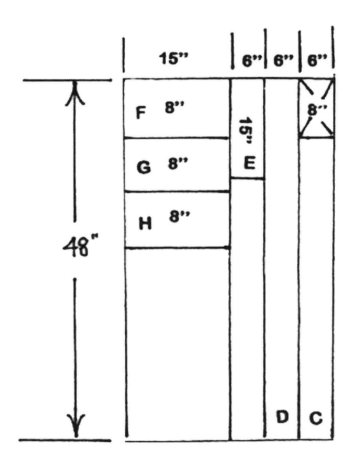

WE START BY BUILDING THE MAIN MEMBER.
TAKE PART "D" AND "C". MARK ONE END OF PART "D" WITH A 45° ANGLE ON
IT'S SIDE.

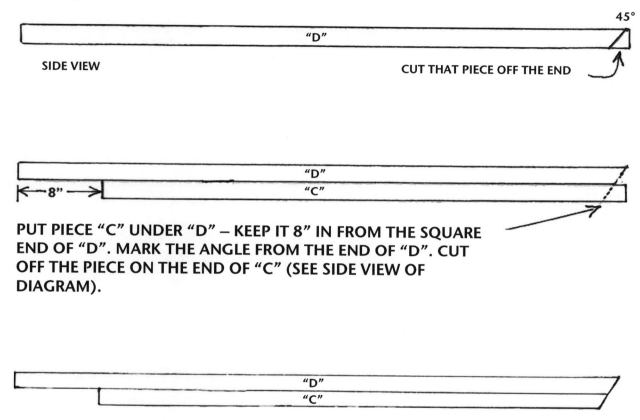

PUT PIECE "C" UNDER "D" – KEEP IT 8" IN FROM THE SQUARE
END OF "D". MARK THE ANGLE FROM THE END OF "D". CUT
OFF THE PIECE ON THE END OF "C" (SEE SIDE VIEW OF
DIAGRAM).

KEEP THEM IN POSITION – USE ELMERS WOOD GLUE – GLUE AND NAIL
THEM TOGETHER. USE 1" FINISHING NAILS.

THIS WILL GIVE YOU THE MAIN MEMBER OF YOUR SHIRT PRINTER.

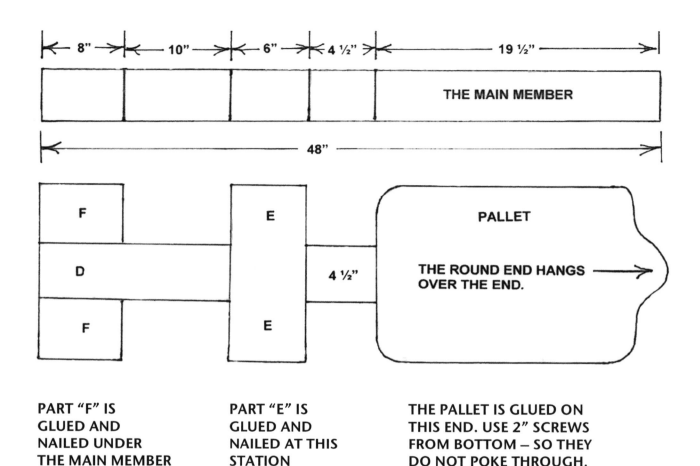

|← 8" →|← 10" →|← 6" →|← 4 ½" →|← 19 ½" →|

THE MAIN MEMBER

|← 48" →|

F

E

PALLET

D

4 ½"

THE ROUND END HANGS → OVER THE END.

F

E

PART "F" IS GLUED AND NAILED UNDER THE MAIN MEMBER

PART "E" IS GLUED AND NAILED AT THIS STATION

THE PALLET IS GLUED ON THIS END. USE 2" SCREWS FROM BOTTOM – SO THEY DO NOT POKE THROUGH.

MAKE THE PALLET FROM THE FORMICA COATED SINK CUT-OUT. IF ONE IS NOT AVAILABLE, CUT IT OUT OF ¾" EXTERIOR PLYWOOD. COVER IT WITH FORMICA FROM A COUNTERTOP MAKER. HE MIGHT GLUE IT FOR YOU OR EVEN MAKE YOU ONE FROM OUR PATTERN.

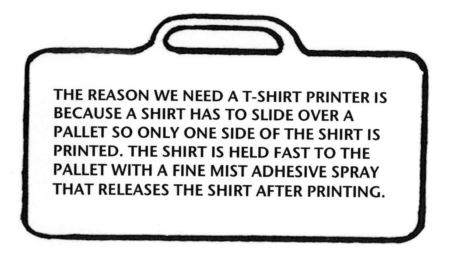

THE REASON WE NEED A T-SHIRT PRINTER IS BECAUSE A SHIRT HAS TO SLIDE OVER A PALLET SO ONLY ONE SIDE OF THE SHIRT IS PRINTED. THE SHIRT IS HELD FAST TO THE PALLET WITH A FINE MIST ADHESIVE SPRAY THAT RELEASES THE SHIRT AFTER PRINTING.

I KNOW WHAT YOU ARE THINKING – "OH MAN, THIS IS A LOT OF WORK" – BUT ANYTHING WORTHWHILE ENTAILS SOME WORK. ONCE IT IS PUT TOGETHER, YOU WILL HAVE EQUIPEMENT THAT LASTS FOR MANY YEARS – ALL THE TIME, MAKING MONEY FOR YOU.

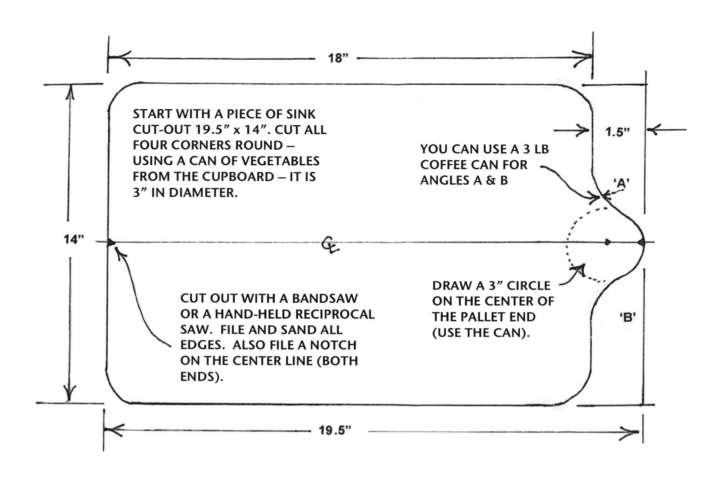

START WITH A PIECE OF SINK CUT-OUT 19.5" x 14". CUT ALL FOUR CORNERS ROUND – USING A CAN OF VEGETABLES FROM THE CUPBOARD – IT IS 3" IN DIAMETER.

YOU CAN USE A 3 LB COFFEE CAN FOR ANGLES A & B

CUT OUT WITH A BANDSAW OR A HAND-HELD RECIPROCAL SAW. FILE AND SAND ALL EDGES. ALSO FILE A NOTCH ON THE CENTER LINE (BOTH ENDS).

DRAW A 3" CIRCLE ON THE CENTER OF THE PALLET END (USE THE CAN).

18"

1.5"

'A'

14"

'B'

19.5"

LAYOUT FOR SHIRT PRINTER PALLET

GLUE PIECES "G" AND "H" TOGETHER AND C-CLAMP THEM AND NAIL.
THIS UNIT IS THE SCREEN HOLDER.

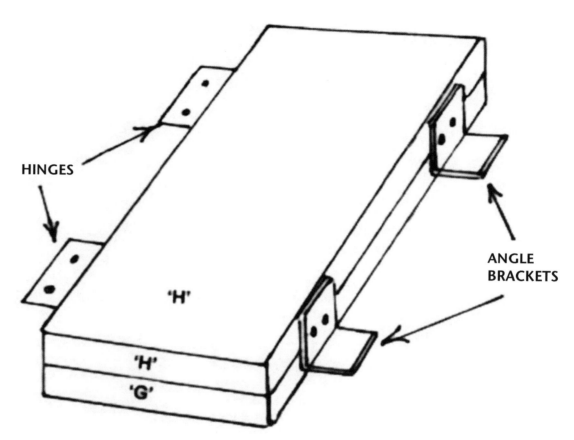

HINGES

ANGLE
BRACKETS

'H'

'H'

'G'

THE ANGLE BRACKETS ARE SHOWN
ON THE SCREEN HOLDER. SEE PG 11
AND 12 ON HOW TO PLACE THEM
ON THE SCREEN HOLDER.

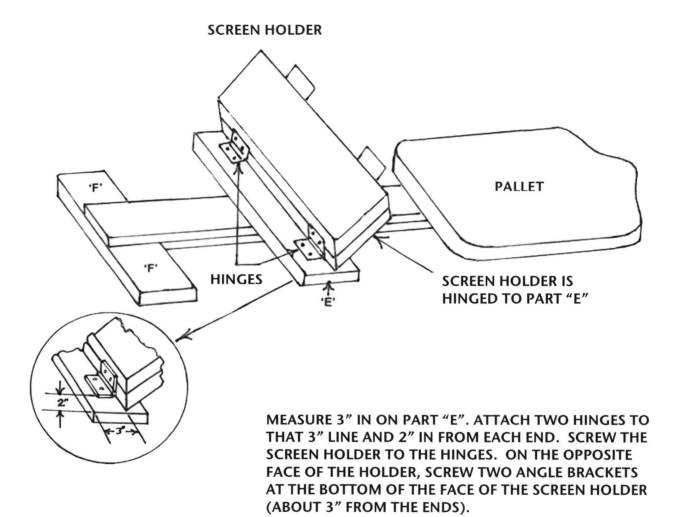

SCREEN HOLDER

'F'

'F'

PALLET

HINGES

'E'

SCREEN HOLDER IS
HINGED TO PART "E"

2"

3"

MEASURE 3" IN ON PART "E". ATTACH TWO HINGES TO
THAT 3" LINE AND 2" IN FROM EACH END. SCREW THE
SCREEN HOLDER TO THE HINGES. ON THE OPPOSITE
FACE OF THE HOLDER, SCREW TWO ANGLE BRACKETS
AT THE BOTTOM OF THE FACE OF THE SCREEN HOLDER
(ABOUT 3" FROM THE ENDS).

SEE NEXT PAGE FOR ILLUSTRATION.

INSTALL TWO ANGLE BRACKETS ON
THE FACE OF THE SCREEN HOLDER.

INSTALL ANGLE BRACKETS LEVEL WITH THE
PALLET SURFACE.

PLACE A PIECE OF PLYWOOD SO THE
SCREEN HOLDER ASSEMBLY RESTS ON IT.

TAPE A PIECE OF SHO CARD ON THE
PALLET SO IT BUMPS THE FACE OF THE
SCREEN HOLDER.

POSITION THE ANGLE BRACKET 3" FROM THE END. MARK THE SCREW HOLES.

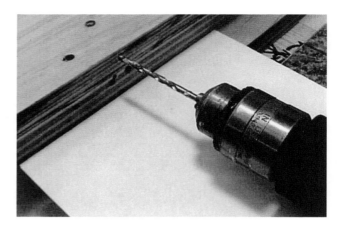

DRILL THE MARKED HOLES WITH A 1/16" DRILL.
(YOU CAN LIFT UP THE HOLDER TO DRILL)

BOTH SIDES OF THE MAIN MEMBER GET ANGLE HOLD-DOWN BRACKETS.

HOW THE ANGLE BRACKETS HOLD DOWN THE FRONT OF THE MAIN MEMBER.

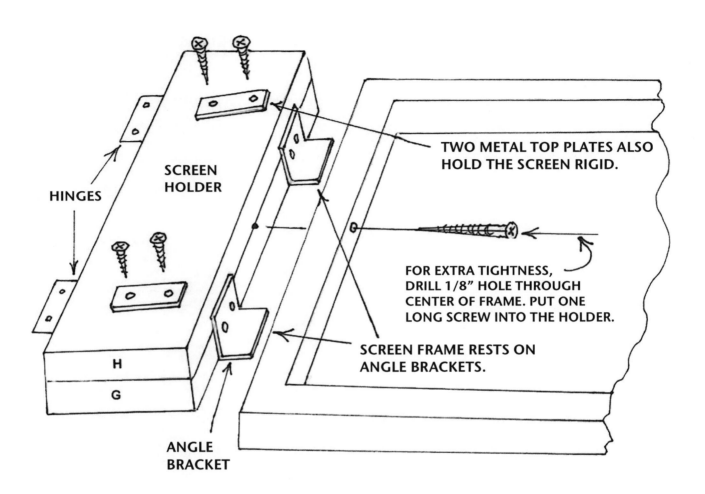

HINGES

SCREEN HOLDER

H

G

ANGLE BRACKET

TWO METAL TOP PLATES ALSO HOLD THE SCREEN RIGID.

FOR EXTRA TIGHTNESS, DRILL 1/8" HOLE THROUGH CENTER OF FRAME. PUT ONE LONG SCREW INTO THE HOLDER.

SCREEN FRAME RESTS ON ANGLE BRACKETS.

COUNTER WEIGHT BRACKET IS MADE FROM 1" x 30" x 1/8" THICK STEEL FLAT STOCK.
DRILL TWO 1/8" HOLES SPACED 4" APART AT THE 11" END. BEND AT MEASURED LENGTHS.

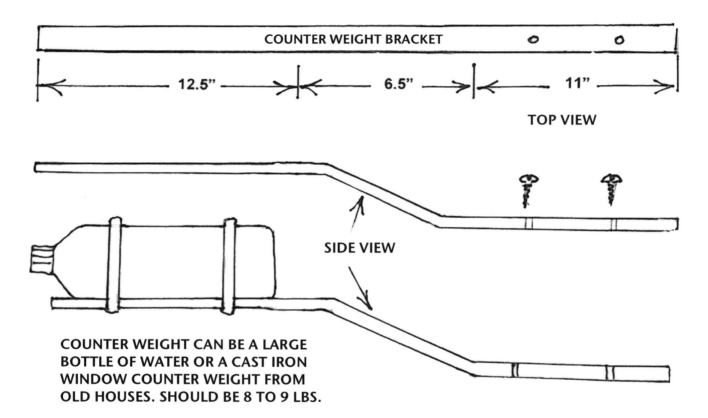

COUNTER WEIGHT BRACKET

12.5" — 6.5" — 11"

TOP VIEW

SIDE VIEW

COUNTER WEIGHT CAN BE A LARGE
BOTTLE OF WATER OR A CAST IRON
WINDOW COUNTER WEIGHT FROM
OLD HOUSES. SHOULD BE 8 TO 9 LBS.

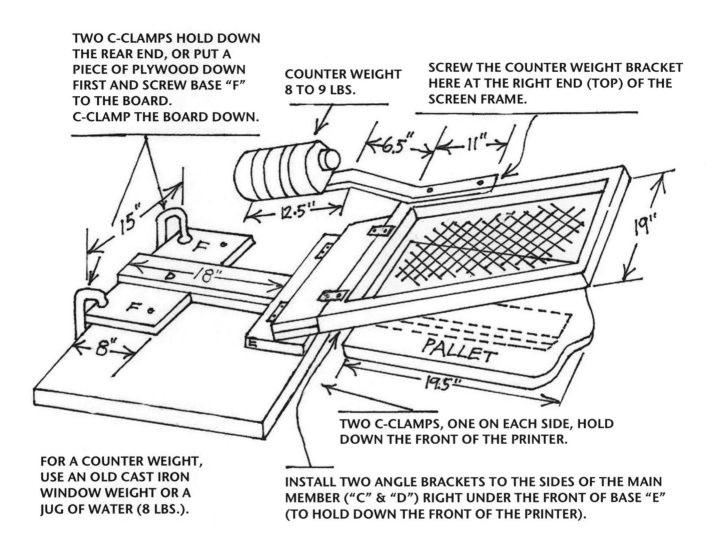

TWO C-CLAMPS HOLD DOWN THE REAR END, OR PUT A PIECE OF PLYWOOD DOWN FIRST AND SCREW BASE "F" TO THE BOARD.
C-CLAMP THE BOARD DOWN.

COUNTER WEIGHT 8 TO 9 LBS.

SCREW THE COUNTER WEIGHT BRACKET HERE AT THE RIGHT END (TOP) OF THE SCREEN FRAME.

6.5" 11"

12.5"

15"

19"

F

D 18"

F

8"

PALLET

19.5"

FOR A COUNTER WEIGHT, USE AN OLD CAST IRON WINDOW WEIGHT OR A JUG OF WATER (8 LBS.).

TWO C-CLAMPS, ONE ON EACH SIDE, HOLD DOWN THE FRONT OF THE PRINTER.

INSTALL TWO ANGLE BRACKETS TO THE SIDES OF THE MAIN MEMBER ("C" & "D") RIGHT UNDER THE FRONT OF BASE "E" (TO HOLD DOWN THE FRONT OF THE PRINTER).

63

CHAPTER SEVEN
WE PRINT A T-SHIRT ON OUR PRINTER

STAND YOUR PREPARED SCREEN ON END, WITH THE BOTTOM OF THE IMAGE ON TOP.

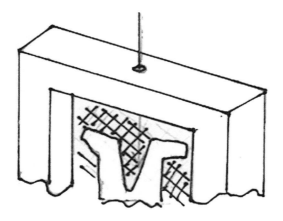

WITH THE PALLET HANGING OVER THE TABLE EDGE, THE PRINTER IS C-CLAMPED TO THE TABLE. BRING DOWN THE HINGED SCREEN HOLDER. THEN PLACE THE SCREEN ON THE PALLET. SLIDE THE SCREEN UP TO THE FACE OF THE SCREEN HOLDER SO THAT THE SCREEN IS RESTING ON THE TWO ANGLE BRACKETS. SCREW THE 2" CENTER SCREW IN PLACE.

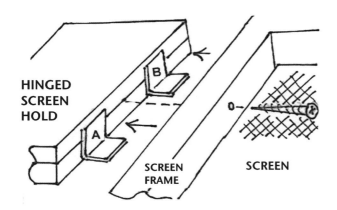

HINGED SCREEN HOLD

SCREEN FRAME

SCREEN

THE SCREEN RESTS ON ANGLE BRACKETS "A" & "B", WITH THE 2" SCREW HOLDING THE SCREEN.

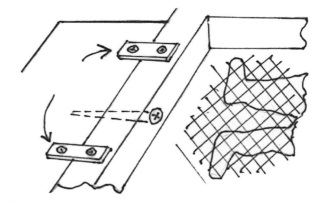

TWO TOP FLAT METAL BRACKETS HOLD THE SCREEN AGAINST THE HOLDER.

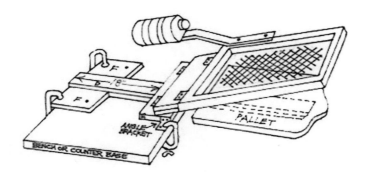

WITH THE SCREEN ATTACHED, WE ARE ABOUT READY TO PRINT.

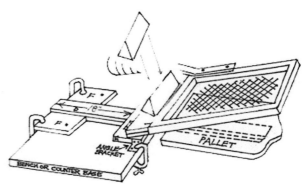

ADD A CARDBOARD REST ON THE SCREEN FRAME FOR THE SQUEEGE.

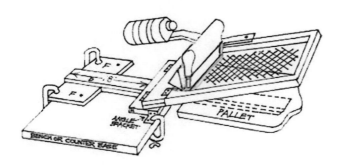

PLACE THE SQUEEGE AGAINST THE REST.

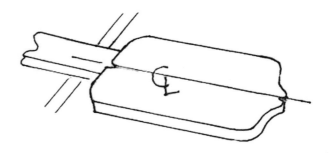

DRAW A CENTER LINE ON THE PALLET USING THE CENTER NOTCHES ON EACH END.

SPRAY THE PALLET WITH SPRAY STICK AND LET IT DRY. SLIDE THE T-SHIRT OVER THE PALLET. USE THE CENTER CREASE ON THE SHIRT TO LINE IT UP ON THE PALLET. WITH THE SCREEN IN THE UP POSITION, PUT SPECIAL PRODUCT INK ON THE SCREEN — IN FRONT OF THE SQUEEGE.

PUSH THE SHIRT EVENLY ON THE PALLET.

LAY YOUR BLANK SHIRTS WITH THE NECK HOLE TOWARDS YOU. MAKE SURE YOU PRINT ON THE SIDE YOUR CUSTOMER WANTS. ALWAYS CHECK YOUR HANDS FOR INK (AS YOU PRINT).

SPECIAL PRODUCT INKS ARE OIL-BASED. THEY AIR-DRY AND STAY FLEXIBLE.

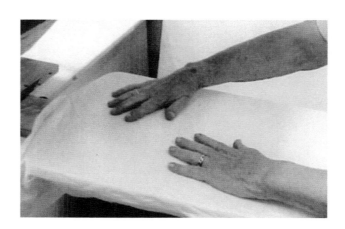

CHECK FINGERS FOR PAINT. SMOOTH THE SHIRT WITH YOUR HANDS.

HEY! WHAT IS THIS SHIRT DOING HERE?

WITH BOTH HANDS, PULL THE SQUEEGE TOWARDS YOU IN A PRINTING STROKE.

AT THE END OF THE STROKE, PICK UP SOME PAINT WITH THE SQUEEGE AND PULL A SECOND STROKE.

LIFT THE SCREEN AND PUSH THE PAINT BACK FOR A FLOOD COAT ON THE SCREEN.

LIFT THE SCREEN TO SEE YOUR HANDY WORK.

USE WOODEN SNAP CLOTHES PINS TO HANG THE SHIRTS UP.

THIS SHIRT PRINT CAN LAST FOR YEARS — MAKING MONEY.

THE NEXT PAGE IS A SUMMARY OF HOW TO PREPARE AND SET UP A SCREEN FOR THE SHIRT PRINTER.

LATER ON I'LL SHOW YOU HOW TO PRINT MULTICOLOR SHIRTS.

TO SUMMARIZE

BEFORE YOU SPRAY THE PALLET, YOUR SCREEN ART SHOULD BE A FILM POSITIVE (BLACK LETTERS AND ART ON A FILM TRANSPARENCY). LAY THE ART ON THE PALLET CENTER LINE, WHERE YOU WANT IT ON THE SHIRT. HOLD IT DOWN WITH TINY PIECES OF MASKING TAPE. * REMEMBER THE SHIRT BOTTOM IS AWAY FROM YOU ON THE PALLET.

NOW TURN ON THE YELLOW LIGHT AND TURN OFF THE OTHER LIGHTS. PULL DOWN THE SHADES. MOUNT YOUR COATED-OUT SCREEN ON THE PRESS WITH JUST THE CENTER SCREW. PUT PIECES OF SCOTCH-TAPE (UPSIDE DOWN) UNDER THE EDGES OF THE FILM ART. TAKE AWAY THE MASKING TAPE PIECES.

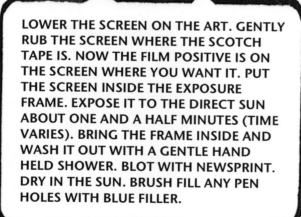

LOWER THE SCREEN ON THE ART. GENTLY RUB THE SCREEN WHERE THE SCOTCH TAPE IS. NOW THE FILM POSITIVE IS ON THE SCREEN WHERE YOU WANT IT. PUT THE SCREEN INSIDE THE EXPOSURE FRAME. EXPOSE IT TO THE DIRECT SUN ABOUT ONE AND A HALF MINUTES (TIME VARIES). BRING THE FRAME INSIDE AND WASH IT OUT WITH A GENTLE HAND HELD SHOWER. BLOT WITH NEWSPRINT. DRY IN THE SUN. BRUSH FILL ANY PEN HOLES WITH BLUE FILLER.

MAKIN' MONEY

CHAPTER EIGHT

CLEAN THE SCREEN AFTER THE JOB IS PRINTED

(AND RE-CLAIM THE INK)

READ THE BOOK, THEN REMEMBER THIS... TO GET STARTED AND MAKE MONEY, YOU ONLY NEED THE BASIC PRINTING BOARD, SCREEN AND SQUEEGE. DON'T WORRY ABOUT THE SCREEN PREPARATION — YOU GET THE ART FROM THE CUSTOMER, OR HAVE IT DONE BY A FRIEND, OR SEND IT TO GEORGE AND FRANCISCO IN L.A. THEY WILL MAKE THE SCREEN FOR YOU.

CONCENTRATE ON ONE-COLOR JOBS TO START.

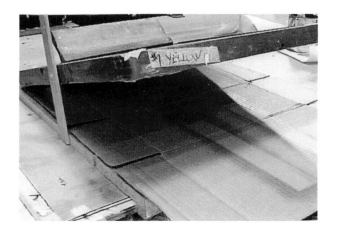

PUT A PIECE OF CARDBOARD BOX ON THE PRINTING AREA.

THEN A COUPLE LAYERS OF NEWSPRINT PAPER.

PULL THE INK TOWARDS YOU SO YOU CAN RECLAIM IT.

CLEAN THE SQUEEGE WITH A RAG & APPROPRIATE THINNER.

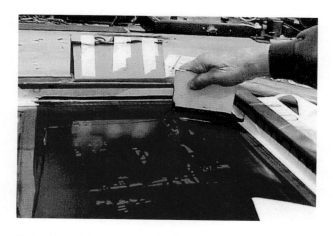

SAVE THE INK FOR ANOTHER JOB.

STILL SAVING THE INK.

FOR ENAMEL AND POSTER INK, USE MINERAL SPIRITS FOR CLEANUP.

USE RAGS AND RUBBER GLOVES AND CHANGE NEWSPRINT OCCASSIONALLY.

WHEN CLEAN, RUB BOTH SIDES WITH LACQUER THINNER. IT HAS TO BE CLEAN — NO SMOKING.

IF THE JOB IS FINISHED, YOU CAN RECLAIM THE SCREEN.

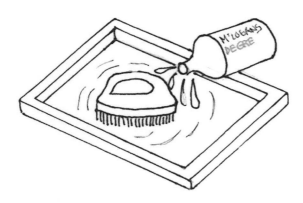

LAY THE SCREEN FACE DOWN IN A SINK. ADD SCREEN RECLAIMER SOLUTION AND LIGHTLY SCRUB WITH A BRUSH.

LET IS SET FOR FIVE MINUTES THEN FLUSH WITH A POWER SPRAYER.

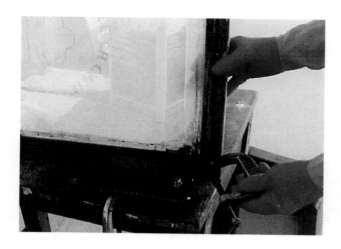

USE A PIECE OF WOOD AND C-CLAMPS TO HOLD THE SCREEN.

WE WASH THE SCREEN OUTSIDE USING RUBBER GLOVES AND LACQUER THINNER.

CHANGE THE RAGS – RUB UNTIL THE SCREEN IS CLEAN.

CLEAN THE SCREEN. ONCE DRY, IT CAN BE WET SANDED WITH 600 GRIT WET SANDPAPER.

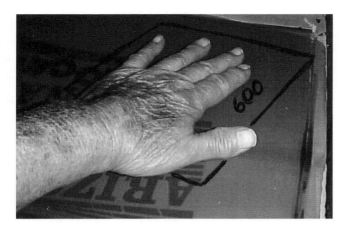

WET SAND THE PRINTING SIDE OF THE
SILK WITH 600 GRIT WET SANDPAPER.

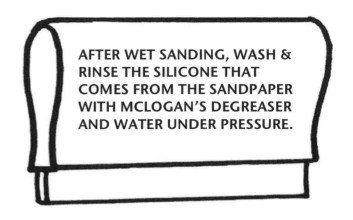

AFTER WET SANDING, WASH &
RINSE THE SILICONE THAT
COMES FROM THE SANDPAPER
WITH MCLOGAN'S DEGREASER
AND WATER UNDER PRESSURE.

RINSE THE DEGREASER OUT WITH A STRONG
SPRAY. LET DRY.

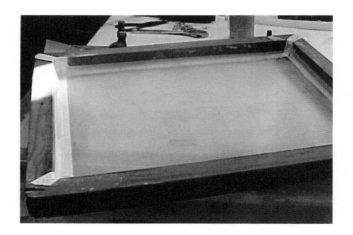

CLEAN SCREEN READY TO USE AGAIN,
JUST COAT IT OUT.

CHAPTER NINE
SERVICES AND TECH SUPPORT

OUR WEBSITE
www.goldmineinasuitcase.com
Visit our site for ongoing updates/additions to this book.

McLOGAN
www.mclogan.com
2010 S. Main St.
Los Angeles, CA 90007
Screen Printing Supplies
Many locations in the West. Call 1-213-749-2262
Ask a Question – They have the Answer

"SAL" at DAYTON WEST
174 E. Bellvue
Pasadena, CA 91105
1-626-449-5303
Photo work, makes film positives from your art

EXPOSED TO ART
15828 S. Broadway, Unit D
Gardena, CA 90248
1-310-965-1902, George and Francisco
Send your art – they do the rest.
All photo work, make screens to your order – large or small.

Diploma

This is to certify that

_____

Has successfully completed
Bob Licher's 1st course in
photo screen printing

ILLUSTRATION OF A SAMPLE JOB

1. TALK OVER ORDER WITH CUSTOMER
2. GET DEPOSIT FROM CUSTOMER TO COVER COST OF SHIRTS, SCREEN, ART/PHOTO CHARGES
3. ORDER SHIRTS
4. TYPE SET ON MYLAR WITH FORMAT LETTERS — HAVE ANY ARTWORK PHOTOGRAPHED FOR FILM POSITIVE
5. STRIP IN ART AND TYPE
6. USE PROPER INK FOR EACH JOB TYPE: DECALS — LACQUER, ENAMEL, T-SHIRTS — PERMA FLEX INK PX SERIES (AIR DRIES)
7. CURE SCREEN IN SUN
8. SET ART (FILM POSITIVE) ON PALLET — LINE UP WITH CENTERLINE — PUT MASKING TAPE UPWARDS
9. PLACE COATED SCREEN IN HOLDER ON PRESS — LOCK IN PLACE
10. BRING DOWN SCREEN TO MYLAR FILM — RUB DOWN SO TAPE HOLDS THE MYLAR IMAGE TO THE SCREEN'S BOTTOM FACE
11. TAKE SCREEN OUT OF PRESS, EXCHANGE MASKING TAPE WITH SCOTCH TAPE
12. EXPOSE SCREEN TO ULTRA-VIOLET LIGHT UNDER FLAT GLASS (SUNLIGHT FOR AROUND ONE AND A HALF MINUTES) — DON'T OVER EXPOSE, IT WON'T WASH OUT — TAKE MYLAR OFF
13. WASH OUT SCREEN FIRST WITH COLD WATER FOR 30 SECONDS — THEN HOT WATER
14. DRY THE SCREEN — CURE IN SUNLIGHT — TOUCH UP SCREEN BY FILLING ANY HOLES WITH BLUE FILLER
15. TAPE INSIDE CORNERS TO PREVENT LEAKS
16. USE SPECIAL PRODUCT INK — IT AIR DRIES
17. SECURE SCREEN IN THE PRESS
18. ADD INK AND SQUEEGE TO THE SCREEN
19. SPRAY SPRAY-STICK TO THE PALLET SURFACE (TO HOLD THE SHIRT IN PLACE) — PUT SHIRT ON THE PALLET
20. BRING SCREEN DOWN ON TO THE SHiRT — PULL SQUEEGE AND PRINT THE SHIRT

CHAPTER TEN

PRINT THE COVER OF THIS BOOK

USING THE BASIC SETUP, YOU CAN PRINT MULTI-COLOR WORKS LIKE THIS BOOK COVER

START WITH A FINISHED BLACK AND WHITE RENDERING OF THE COVER ON CARD STOCK. THIS BLACK AND WHITE RENDERING ON CARD STOCK – MOUNTED ON THE BASE CARD – WILL BE OUR SET UP CARD WITH REGISTER MARKS TO RUN THE WHOLE 4-COLOR JOB.

TAKE THE FINISHED BLACK AND WHITE RENDERING TO STAPLES, KINKOS OR SIMILAR STORE. MAKE TWO FILM TRANSPARENCIES. CUT THE CORNERS OFF ONE. USING A WINDOW OR LIGHT TABLE, LAY ONE ON TOP OF THE OTHER, LINE THE IMAGES UP, THEN SCOTCH-TAPE THEM TOGETHER. USE THIS FILM TO EXPOSE YOUR BLACK SCREEN.

WE LEARNED HOW TO EXPOSE AND DEVELOP SCREENS IN CHAPTER FIVE. USE THE SAME TECHNIQUE TO MAKE THE BLACK SCREEN.

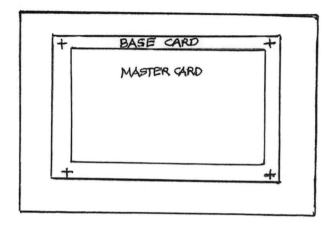

ADD FOUR REGISTER MARKS ON ALL FOUR CORNERS OF THE BASE CARD.

THEY HAVE A STICKY BACK, BUT SCOTCH-TAPE THEM SO THEY STAY PUT. REGISTER MARKS ARE VERY IMPORTANT. YOU WILL USE THEM TO LINE UP ALL OF YOUR COLORS.

THE BASE BOARD IS MADE FROM .050" THICK SHO CARD. I USE SILK BOARD – IT IS STABLE AND HAS COATED PAPER ON BOTH SIDES. THE BASE BOARD SHOULD BE ONE INCH LARGER THAN THE SIZE OF YOUR BOOK COVER.

WITH A LIGHT SPRAY OF ELMERS SPRAY GLUE, MOUNT THE MASTER CARD ONE INCH IN – ALL AROUND – ON THE BASE CARD. THIS IS OUR MASTER LAYOUT CARD.

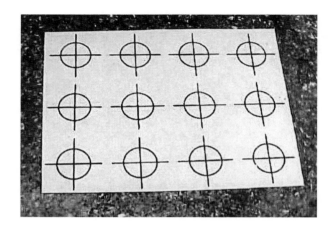

TAKE ONE OF THE PAPER COPIES OF THE BLACK AND WHITE LAYOUT. WITH COLORED PENCILS, COLOR IN AREAS YOU WANT FOR THE FINISHED COVER. USE THIS AS A GUIDE TO CUT AMBERLITH COLOR SEPARATIONS. YOU WILL EXPOSE THE DIFFERENT COLOR SCREENS WITH THESE SEPARATIONS.

MAKE YOUR OWN REGISTER MARKS

DRAW A BLOCK OF REGISTER MARKS, THEN DUPLICATE THEM ON A PRINTER. PASTE A GROUP OF REGISTER MARKS ON A SHEET. MAKE FOUR TRANSPARENCIES AT STAPLES OR KINKOS. SPRAY THE BACK OF THE SHEETS WITH ELMERS SPRAY STICK. MOUNT THEM ON WAX PAPER. CUT OUT AND USE AS NEEDED.

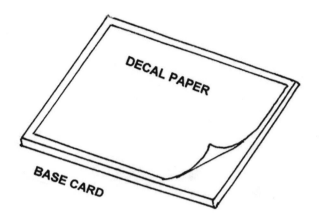

DECAL PAPER

BASE CARD

I CHOSE TO PRINT ON 8.5" X 8.5" COVER STOCK, THAT WAS CENTER MOUNTED ON A PIECE OF SILK BOARD FOR A REASON. THIS IS THE WAY TO PRINT DECALS. PAPER MOUNTED ON CARD IS EASY TO REGISTER.

YOU ALWAYS MARK THE FIRST CARD AS A SET UP CARD THAT WAY THE REGISTER GUIDES ARE THE SAME FOR EACH COLOR YOU RUN.

PRINTING SLIDE OFF DECALS

LACQUER DECAL PAPER IS COATED WITH GELATIN EMULSION THAT ABSORBS MOISTURE FROM THE AIR, CAUSING THE PAPER TO CURL AND MAKING IT HARD TO REGISTER. MOUNTING THE PAPER CARDS MEANS EVERY PIECE IS PERFECT.

TAKE CAUTION USING SPRAY STICK ON CARRYING CARDS – TOO MUCH AND YOU CAN'T REMOVE THE DECAL PAPER AFTER IT IS PRINTED. JUST LIGHTLY SPRAY THE CARRYING CARD. LET DRY. A LIGHT TAC IS ALL YOU WANT.

WHEN PRINTING DECALS, THE BASE CARD IS JUST A HAIR OR TWO LARGER THAN THE PAPER, SO YOU CAN'T SPRAY THE PAPER – IT HAS TO BE POURUS TO LET WATER THROUGH THE PAPER TO SOFTEN THE GELATIN AND RELEASE THE DECAL.

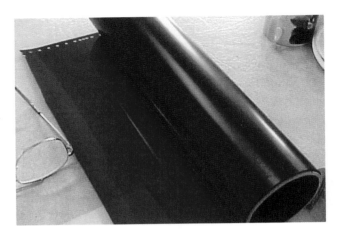

AMBERLITH LACQUER FILM FOR MAKING COLOR SEPARATION FILM POSITIVES.

TAPE A PIECE OF AMBERLITH OVER THE ENTIRE MASTER CARD.

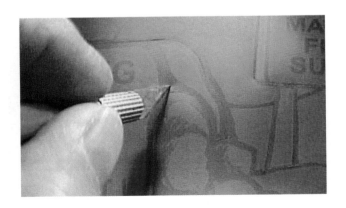

CUT AND PEEL THE LACQUER FILM FOR THE BLUE SKY RIGHT ON THE LINES.

PEEL OFF THE EXCESS FILM LEAVING THE RED FILM FOR THE BLUE SKY.

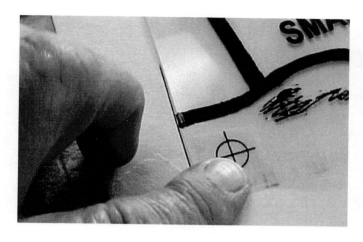

PLACE REGISTER MARKS OVER THE MASTER CARD REGISTER MARKS. SCOTCH-TAPE THEM DOWN.

LEAVE THE FILM ON THE SPACE (BLUE SKY) YOU WANT TO PRINT.

YOU NEED ONE SHEET OF AMBERLITH FILM FOR EACH COLOR. NOW YOU HAVE A FILM POSITIVE ON THE CARD.

WITH MATCHING REGISTER MARKS YOU "SHOOT" OR EXPOSE A SILK SCREEN IMAGE WITH THE TRANSPARENCY.

WITH THE REGISTER MARKS LINED UP, TAPE THE BLUE SKY FILM TO THE SET UP MASTER CARD. TAPE A PUSH CARD (4x8) TO THE RIGHT SIDE OF THE CARD.

SLIP A PIECE OF WHITE PAPER UNDER THE FILM POSITIVE SO ONLY THE RED IMAGE ON THE AMBERLITH SHOWS.

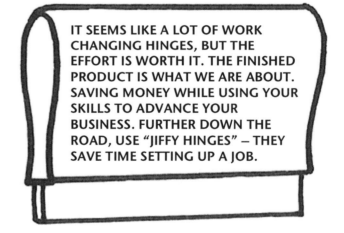

IT SEEMS LIKE A LOT OF WORK CHANGING HINGES, BUT THE EFFORT IS WORTH IT. THE FINISHED PRODUCT IS WHAT WE ARE ABOUT. SAVING MONEY WHILE USING YOUR SKILLS TO ADVANCE YOUR BUSINESS. FURTHER DOWN THE ROAD, USE "JIFFY HINGES" – THEY SAVE TIME SETTING UP A JOB.

TO SAVE MONEY, WE USE SIMPLE HINGES. EACH SET UP REQUIRES YOU MOVE SCREENS.

AFTER CUTTING THE SKY BLUE FILM POSITIVE, I CUT AND PEELED THE SECOND COLOR – GOLDEN YELLOW.

SO THE TOPS OF THE IMAGES WERE BUTTING INTO EACH OTHER.

PICTURE OF 2 IMAGE SCREEN.
** IMPORTANT! TAPE PAPER OVER LOWER IMAGE BEFORE PRINTING SKY. AFTER PRINTING, CLEAN SCREEN AND BLOCK OUT SKY BEFORE PRINTING BOTTOM IMAGE.

REPEAT THE AMBERLITH FILM FOR EACH COLOR, SO YOU HAVE FILM TRANSPARENCIES FOR ALL COLORS WITH REGISTER MARKS ON ALL FOUR CORNERS.

EXPOSE ALL SCREENS AND WASH OUT.

ATTACH THE FIRST SCREEN TO THE PRINTING BORAD WITH HINGES AND ATTACH THE HOLD UP STICK.

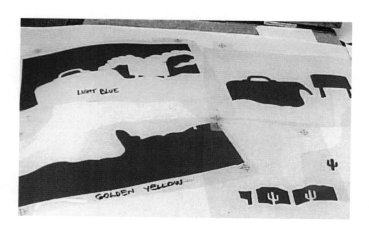

AMBERLITH CUT OUTS ON CLEAR POLYESTER CARRYING SHEETS FOR EACH COLOR, WITH REGISTER MARKS.

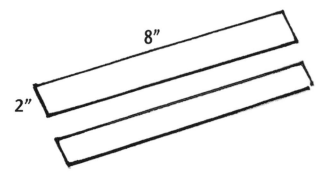

LOWER THE SCREEN AND MANUEVER THE MASTER CARD TO LINE UP THE CARD IMAGE WITH THE SCREEN IMAGE.

CUT TWO PIECES OF SHO CARD FOR REGISTER GUIDES. SPRAY ONE SIDE WITH ELMER'S SPRAY STICK.

LET THE TWO GUDES DRY FOR A WHILE. RAISE THE SCREEN WHILE YOU HOLD DOWN THE ALIGNED MASTER CARD.

PLACE THE TWO GUIDES, STICKY SIDE DOWN, ONE ON THE LEFT OF THE MASTER CARD, ONE ON THE BOTTOM OF THE MASTER CARD.

DO NOT MOVE THE MASTER CARD AS YOU NUZZLE THE GUIDES INTO PLACE.

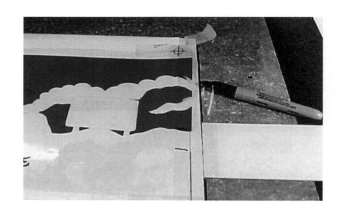

WITH A BLACK MARKER, OUTLINE THE RIGHT AND BOTTOM OF THE MASTER CARD ON THE PRINT BOARD.

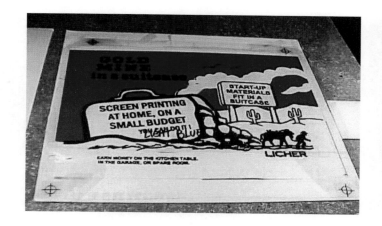

MOVE THE MASTER CARD AWAY FROM THE GUIDES. PUT THE CARD AGAINST THE GUIDES, LOWER THE SCREEN TO LOOK AND MAKE SURE THE SCREEN STILL LINES UP WITH THE IMAGE ON THE CARD. IF NOT, REMOVE THE GUIDES AND RE-DO THE PROCESS UNTIL IT LINES UP. PUT MASKING TAPE ON THE ENDS OF THE GUIDES.

USE THE OUTLINE OF THE CARD AND THE TWO GUIDES TO MASK THE OUTER SURFACE OF THE PRINTING BOARD WITH NEWSPRINT AND MASKING TAPE, LEAVING THE CARD AREA OPEN.

SPRAY THE OPEN AREA LIGHTLY WITH ELMER'S SPRAY STICK.

WAFF THE GLUE WITH A CARD AND REMOVE THE NEWSPRINT. THE SPRAY STICK WILL HOLD THE CARD IN PLACE.

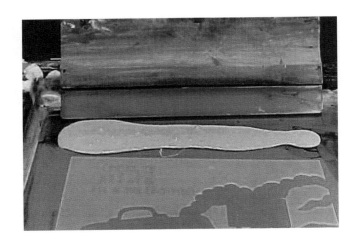

LOWER THE SCREEN. WITH A STEADY PULL AND PRESSURE — DRAW THE SQUEEGE TOWARDS YOU IN A PRINTING STROKE.

POUR THE PAINT ACROSS THE SCREEN IN FRONT OF THE SQUEEGE. LIFT THE SCREEN AND PULL THE PAINT ACROSS THE IMAGE ON THE SCREEN TO CHARGE THE SCREEN WITH A FLOOD COAT.

AT THE END OF THE PRINTING STROKE, LIFT THE SCREEN AND PUSH THE PAINT BACK ACROSS THE SCREEN FOR A FLOOD COAT.

REST THE SQUEEGE ON IT'S CARD-BOARD REST. PROP UP THE SCREEN WITH THE PAINT STICK ATTACHED TO THE LEFT SIDE OF THE SCREEN FRAME. REMOVE THE PRINTED CARD AND DO ANOTHER UNTIL THE FIRST COLOR IS PRINTED ON ALL THE CARDS.

IF THE SCREEN TOUCHES THE CARD, TAPE ONE OR TWO PIECES OF SILK BOARD ON THE PRINTING BOARD UNDER THE TWO CORNERS OF THE SCREEN FRAME.

THAT WILL HOLD THE SCREEN UP 1/8" FOR "OFF CONTACT" PRINTING. THE SCREEN LIFTS UP AFTER THE SQUEEGE PASSES OVER THE PRINTING STROKE. IT PREVENTS SMUDGING.

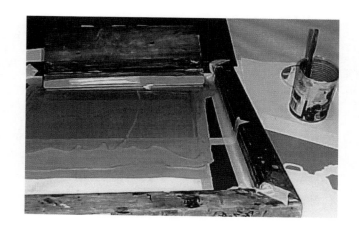

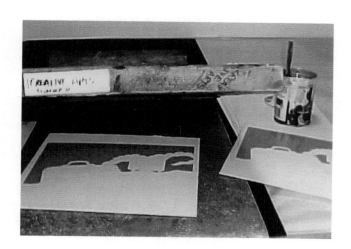

PUT SOME NEWSPRINT ON THE PRINTING BOARD. LOWER THE SCREEN AND PICK UP EXCESS PAINT WITH SOME SILK BOARD.

SAVE THE PAINT — ONE QUART OF SCREEN PAINT (OR INK) CAN PRINT HUNDREDS OF SHORT RUN JOBS.

CLEAN THE SCREEN, TURN IT AROUND FOR THE NEXT COLOR (GOLDEN YELLOW).

REPEAT THE SAME PROCESS FOR EACH COLOR.

PUT NEWSPRINT DOWN AND CLEAN THE SCREEN TO SAVE THE INK.

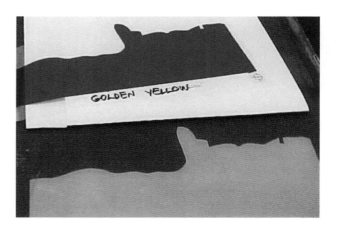

SECOND COLOR IS GOLDEN YELLOW.

POSITION RED FILM ON MASTER CARD. SCOTCH-TAPE IN PLACE.

ADD REGISTER GUIDES LEFT AND BOTTOM.

POUR PAINT, RAISE SCREEN, FLOOD COAT AND PRINT ALL FOUR.

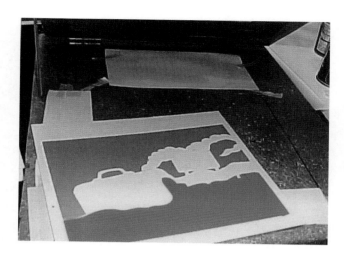

PRINTING THE YELLOW. PRINT ONE OR ONE THOUSAND. IF THESE WERE ART FOR SALE, THERE IS MONEY TO BE MADE.

TWO COLORS PRINTED — ALL GOOD.

NEXT COLOR — MAGENTA FOR DISTANT MOUNTAINS. WHITE PAPER UNDER FOR FILM FOR REGISTERING.

LINE UP THE SCREEN WITH THE FILM POSITIVE.

DON'T FORGET TO LINE UP THE REGISTER MARKS.

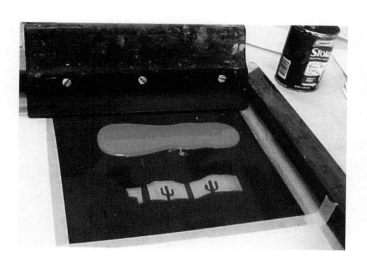

ALL SET UP, POUR THE PAINT AND ADD ANOTHER COLOR.

SET UP BEIGE COLOR FOR SUITCASE AND SIGN.

PICKING OUT COLOR AND MIXING COLOR FOR THE SUITCASE.

MIXING A COLOR USING THE COLOR GUIDE.

WHITE PAPER UNDER FILM FOR LINE UP AND SETTING GUIDES.

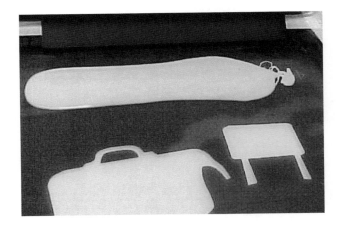

HERE IS COLOR ON THE SCREEN READY TO GO.

NEWSPRINT AND PAPER FOR CLEANUP.

WHITE PAPER UNDER FILM FOR LINE UP AND SETTING GUIDES.

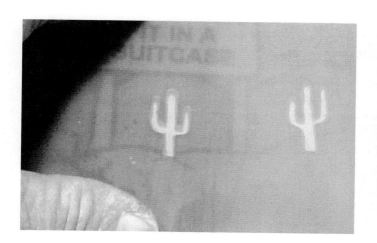

LINE UP THE SCREEN WITH THE FILM POSITIVE.

SET THE GUIDES, BLOCK OUT THE SCREEN TO PRINT GREEN.

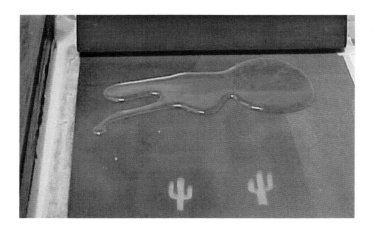

PAINT ON THE SCREEN - - - LET'S PRINT.

WHITE PAPER UNDER FILM FOR LINE UP AND SETTING GUIDES

SLIDE WHITE PAPER UNDER FILM TO LINE UP THE SCREEN.

FLOOD COAT AND LOWER THE SCREEN. PRINT ALL FOUR PIECES.

Made in the USA
Charleston, SC
15 December 2014